D0619453

ICE CREAM

Copyright © 1989 American Teacher Publications

Published by Raintree Publishers Limited Partnership

Library of Congress number: 89-3931

Library of Congress Cataloging in Publication Data.

Keller, Stella.
  The story of ice cream / Stella Keller.

  (Real readers)
  Summary: The anecdotal history of ice cream, for beginning readers, traces the treat from the ices eaten by Emperor Nero to modern day ice cream factories.
    1. Ice cream, ices, etc.—Juvenile literature. [1. Ice cream, ices, etc.] I. Title.
II. Series.
TX795.K45 1989 637'.4—dc20   89-3931

ISBN 0-8172-3523-X

1 2 3 4 5 6 7 8 9 0   93 92 91 90 89

REAL READERS

ICE CREAM

by Stella Keller

illustrated by John Holm

Raintree Publishers

Milwaukee

Ice cream is fun to eat. Today, when you want to eat ice cream, you can go to a store and get it.

Long ago, people did not have good ways to get ice. They did not have **freezers** to keep things cold. For a long time it was so hard to make cold treats, that just kings and queens got to eat them.

How did people of long ago make ice cream and other cold treats?

This is how they did it.

About 2,000 years ago, a man named Nero was the Emperor in Rome. Nero wanted to eat a cold treat.

How did Nero get his cold treat?

There was ice on the tops of the hills outside Rome. Nero would send people to get the ice. After they got the ice, they would run all the way back to Rome. Then Nero's cooks mixed the ice with **fruit** and **honey**.

It was not ice cream. But Nero liked this cold treat very much.

Other people in other places liked to eat cold treats, too. About 700 years ago, a man named Marco Polo went on a trip from his home in Italy. He went to China.

In China, he got to eat something good. It was made with ice, like the treat Nero ate, but it had something new in it. The something new was **milk**. Back then, people in China got milk from an animal called the yak.

How did the people in China make this treat?

They put fruit and **sugar** in a pot. Then they mixed in crushed ice. They added milk. Then they mixed up all the fruit, sugar, milk, and ice.

When Marco Polo went back to Italy, he told his friends all about this new, sweet treat.

About 500 years ago, some cooks in Italy, France, and England made cold, sweet treats. The treats were like the one Marco Polo had in China. But now the cooks added something new.

How did the cooks make the treats?

They added not just milk, but **cream** to ice, fruit, and sugar. They made ice cream!

Back then ice cream was very hard to make. People had to mix the ice, fruit, sugar, and cream for a very, very long time. It was very hard for them to get all the ice they needed to make ice cream and to keep it cold.

Kings and queens got to eat ice cream. Sometimes, the cooks who made the ice cream got to eat a little bit, too. But other people did not get to have ice cream at that time.

Then, about 300 years ago, a man named Procope had a shop in France. Mr. Procope made ice cream in the shop. He made ice cream not just for kings and queens, but for all the people.

How did Mr. Procope make ice cream?

Mr. Procope needed a way to keep lots of ice cream in his shop. He did not have freezers like we do today. But he did have a way to keep ice cream cold. He got big boxes and filled them with ice. The ice helped keep the ice cream cold for a long time.

He made ice cream in many **flavors**. He made **chocolate**, **vanilla**, **strawberry**, and rose-flavored ice cream, too!

As time passed, more and more people got to eat ice cream. At last, ice cream came to America. About 200 years ago, America's first President, George Washington, liked to eat ice cream.

How did people make ice cream in George Washington's time?

First, they mixed the cream, flavors, and sugar in a little pot. Sometimes, they mixed in **eggs**, too. Next, they got a big pot and put ice in it. Then they put the little pot in the big pot.

Two people had to work together. One would beat the mix in the little pot. The other would shake the big pot. It was still very hard to make ice cream!

Then, in 1846, a woman in America made a new **machine** to make ice cream. This woman was named Nancy Johnson.

How did Nancy Johnson make ice cream?

Nancy Johnson's machine had a little pot that fit inside a big pot. The cream mix went in the little pot. The ice went in the big pot. At the top was a crank.

If someone turned the crank, it beat the mix in the little pot and it made the ice in the big pot shake. Now it was not as hard to make ice cream. Many people got ice cream machines. They used the new machines to make ice cream at home.

But soon, people did not have to make ice cream to eat it. In 1851, a man named Jacob Fussell was selling milk and cream in Baltimore. He had too much cream to sell. So, he came up with a plan.

He used the cream that he could not sell to make ice cream. People liked to get ice cream from him. Soon, he was selling more ice cream than cream or milk! He was selling all the ice cream he could make!

How did Jacob Fussell make all the ice cream he needed to sell?

This is how he did it. He got some people together. They used machines like Nancy Johnson's. Many people working together could make lots of ice cream to sell. This was the first ice cream **factory**.

Today, much of the ice cream we eat is made in an ice cream factory. But people can make ice cream at home, too. Some people still make ice cream in machines very much like Nancy Johnson's machine.

Now, you can get ice cream in many places. You can go to a store and get ice cream from the freezer and take it home. You can get an ice cream cone and eat it in a shop. You can make ice cream at home if you have an ice cream machine.

You can eat ice cream in a cup, or in a cone, or on a stick. You can eat it with fruit or with cake. But the best way to eat ice cream is with a friend!

Sharing the Joy of Reading

Beginning readers enjoy reading books on their own. Reading a book is a worthwhile activity in and of itself for a young reader. However, a child's reading can be even more rewarding if it is shared. This sharing can enhance your child's appreciation — both of the book and of his or her own abilities.

- Now that your child has read **Ice Cream**, you can help extend your child's reading experience by encouraging him or her to:

- Retell the story or key concepts presented in this story in his or her own words. The retelling can be oral or written.

- Create a picture of a favorite character, event, or concept from this book.

- Express his or her own ideas and feelings about the subject of this book and other things he or she might want to know about this subject.

Here is an activity that you can do together to help extend your child's appreciation of this book: You and your child can make a sweet-tasting frozen treat. Prepare your child's favorite frozen juice with a little less water than usual. Pour the juice into small paper cups and place the cups in the freezer. When the juice begins to harden, set wooden sticks or plastic spoons in the cups for handles. After the juice solidifies, peel off the paper and enjoy.